salmonpoetry

Publishing Irish & International

Poetry Since 1981

Praise for *Birnam Wood*

"It's possible things are not/ as we wished them to be," José Manuel Cardona *writes in* Birnam Wood, *a superb account of his travels around the world in the service of poetry. Exploring the consequences of the fact that* "Only man is capable of destroying/ what he never created/ and he along believes belong to him," *he creates a rival system of belief, which depends upon his vivid imagery, sophisticated ear, and wisdom borne of experience, all of which his daughter, Hélène, a gifted poet in her own right, has gracefully preserved in her translations. This selection of his poems, spanning the length of an illustrious career, are everything we might wish them to be.*

—CHRISTOPHER MERRILL
author of *Self-Portrait with Dogwood*

Birnam Wood *embodies the self in the world of myth with its attendant themes of tragedy and fate. If the water of exile is longing, the cup brims over in these sun-shattered works of diaspora. Cardona is an essential twentieth-century Spanish poet. His poems journey toward an ever-receding home.*

—MARSHA DE LA O
author of *Antidote for the Night*

The lush and mystical poetry of José Manuel Cardona's Birnam Wood *is firmly rooted in the world of classical mythology as a means of articulating what is human and timeless.*

—BLAS FALCONER
author of *The Foundling Wheel*

From the ghostly amphora that languish at sea bottom "like soft fish that escaped/ the potter's greedy love" to the impulse "to tell how yesterday's solitude was", Hélène Cardona's translations are revelations of language and image, a voice dipped in clear water and wrung through her careful hands.

—DORIANNE LAUX
author of *The Book of Men*

In the best tradition of the Poets of 1927 (including Cernuda and Lorca) and postwar Spanish poetry, José Manuel Cardona, mellifluously renders a typically fine sonnet in his imperially lovely Birnam Wood. *Like the great Spanish poets of his time, he takes from 16th and 17th century poets, from Saint John of the Cross to Luis de Góngora to Antonio Machado and Federico García Lorca. In his lyrical poem to the painter Pedro Bueno, he reveals his command of the sonnet as well as his own daring paradoxical modernity:*

> You pushed the rigor of a limitless art
> to unfathomable mysteries
> opening to the color white the singing
>
> the Chimera never dreamt.
> Occult light, impenetrable aromatic smoke,
> in your paintbrush hands, solitary passion.

—WILLIS BARNSTONE
author of *Mexico in My Heart: New and Selected Poems*

A poetic anthology

Translated from the Spanish
by HÉLÈNE CARDONA

For Andrew,
with deepest
love and gratitude,
Hélène

JOSÉ MANUEL CARDONA

Birnam Wood

El Bosque de Birnam

Published in 2018 by
Salmon Poetry
Cliffs of Moher, County Clare, Ireland
Website: www.salmonpoetry.com
Email: info@salmonpoetry.com

Spanish Text Copyright © 2007 by José Manuel Cardona
English Translation Copyright © 2018 by Hélène Cardona
Originally published in 2007 by the Consell Insular d'Eivissa,
Ibiza, Spain, as *El Bosque de Birnam*

ISBN 978-1-912561-18-6

COVER ARTWORK: *October* by Jacquie Gouveia
www.jgouveia.com
COVER DESIGN & TYPESETTING: *Siobhán Hutson*

Printed in Ireland by Sprint Print

Language is a perpetual orphic song.

— SHELLEY
Prometheus Unbound

Índice

Prólogo de Andrés Neuman   12

I
Poemas a Circe

Poema a Circe II   16
Poema a Circe III   18
Poema a Circe IV   20
Poema a Circe IX   22
Poema a Circe XII   24
Poema a Circe XV   26
Poema a Circe XVII   28
Poema a Circe XVIII   32
Poema a Circe XIX   34
Poema a Circe XX   38

II
El Vendimiador

Ibiza   40
Oda a un joven marino   46
Tom Smithson muerto en su buhardilla   50
El hombre y la piedra   54

Contents

Preface by Andrés Neuman   13

I
Poems to Circe

Poem to Circe II   17
Poem to Circe III   19
Poem to Circe IV   21
Poem to Circe IX   23
Poem to Circe XII   25
Poem to Circe XV   27
Poem to Circe XVII   29
Poem to Circe XVIII   33
Poem to Circe XIX   35
Poem to Circe XX   39

II
The Vintner

Ibiza   43
Ode to a Young Mariner   47
Tom Smithson Dead in his Garret   51
The Man and the Stone   55

III
Otros Poemas

Desde el Ponto Euxino   58
Cimetière de Montrouge   64
El Embeleso   66

CUATRO SONETOS ÓRFICOS
Fuente de la calle de la Hoguera   74
También en soledad de amor herido   76
Entre las azucenas olvidado   78
Al pintor Pedro Bueno en Villa del Río   80

Elegía habitada   82

Agradecimientos   91
Biografía del autor   92
Biografía de la traductora   93

III
Other Poems

From the Euxine Sea   59
Montrouge Cemetery   65
The Spell   67

FOUR ORPHIC SONNETS
Fountain in the Passage of the Bonfire   75
In Solitude Hurt by Love   77
Forgotten Amidst White Lilies   79
To the Painter Pedro Bueno in Villa del Río   81

Inhabited Elegy   83

Acknowledgments   91
About the author   92
About the translator   93

Prólogo

Una de las funciones más altas de la poesía consiste en renovar el asombro de lo elemental, desafiando nuestras inercias e impidiéndonos que hagamos con la vida lo mismo que con la piel; la cual, en las sabias palabras de José Manuel Cardona, es «esa cosa que amamos sin sorpresa/ como una ropa usada cada día».

Se trata de poemas de sólida dicción clásica, agudamente conscientes de las ricas tradiciones que la preceden, donde la mitología, los viajes o la memoria personal representan puntos de partida para la reflexión erótica y metafísica. Tiempo y espacio son materia maleable en manos del autor, cuyo compromiso social se integra con naturalidad en el canto lírico.

Artista multifacética y políglota, Hélène Cardona estaba de algún modo destinada a traducir estos poemas. En palabras de su progenitor: «Llegamos y el milagro se produjo». La emoción de una hija traduciendo a su propio padre — rememorándolo entre líneas, reescribiendo sus palabras, interpretando sus sentidos y silencios — suman vértigo temporal, verdad y emoción a estas bellas traducciones.

—ANDRÉS NEUMAN

Autor de *El viajero del siglo*,
Premio Hiperión de Poesía, National Critics Prize,
2014 Puterbaugh Fellow

Preface

One of the highest functions of poetry is to renew the awe of the elemental, challenging our inertia so we don't take life for granted, the way we do our skin; which, in José Manuel Cardona's wise words, is "The thing we love without surprise/ Like a garment worn every day."

These are poems of solid classical diction, keenly aware of the rich traditions that precede it, where mythology, travel and personal memory represent starting points for erotic and metaphysical reflection. Time and space are malleable matter in the hands of the author, whose social commitment blends naturally into lyrical song.

A multi-faceted and polyglot artist, Hélène Cardona was in some way destined to translate these poems. In her father's words: "We arrived and the miracle happened." The emotion of a daughter translating her own father — remembering him between the lines, rewriting his words, interpreting his sensations and silences — adds impermanent vertigo, truth and emotion to these beautiful translations.

—ANDRÉS NEUMAN
Author of *Traveler of the Century*,
Premio Hiperión de Poesía, National Critics Prize,
2014 Puterbaugh Fellow

I
Poemas a Circe

I
Poems to Circe

Poema a Circe II

Esperanza es tu nombre, porque un nombre
Tiene significados que conoce
Solamente el amor. Enamorado
Beso tu piel de bronce en sol bruñida.
La piel es la corteza de las cosas,
Esa cosa que amamos sin sorpresa
Como una ropa usada cada día.
La piel tiene su aroma, su murmullo,
Su color incendiado y su misterio.
Así el amor empieza por la piel
Por el cabello oscuro, y se penetra
Tal el asta del toro hasta los huesos.
Hasta los huesos, Circe, has penetrado,
Hasta mis huesos anchos que proclaman
El dolor vertebrado de la especie.
Abro en amor mi sangre y te la ofrezco.

Mi gravidez astral de cuadrumano,
De pantera gigante arrodillada,
De pedestal caído y desdentado.
Circe, mis brazos son los que rodean
Tu cuello. Largos brazos que quisieran
Llegar hasta el final más remoto.
Anchas manos de palmas de palmera,
Manos éstas que nunca se han armado,
Propicias al cuchillo y la herida.
Vacías son, no tienen nada. Están
Para lo inútil. De la tierra sólo
Han tomado las flores, no los frutos.
Tú la besas, amor, Circe, deseo.
Tú la besas, las abres y las miras.
¿Preguntas el por qué de su vacío?
Ya ves: aman la tierra que no es suya.

Poem to Circe II

Hope is your name, because a name
Has meanings only love
knows. Enamored
I kiss your bronze skin burnished by sun.
Skin is the bark of things,
The thing we love without surprise
Like a garment worn every day.
Skin has its aroma, its murmur,
Its fiery color and mystery.
Thus love begins with the skin,
With dark hair, and penetrates
Like a bull horn, to the bones.
To the bones, Circe, you've penetrated,
Into my deep bones that proclaim
The vertebrate pain of the species.
I open my blood in love and offer it to you.

My primate astral potency
Of giant panther kneeling,
Of fallen and toothless pedestal.
Circe, it's my arms around your
Neck. Long arms that would reach
the farthest end.
Wide hands with frondlike palms,
These hands were never armed,
Conducive to the knife and wound.
Empty, they hold nothing.
They are for the useless. From the earth
They have only taken flowers, no fruit.
You, my love and desire, Circe, kiss it.
You kiss it, open the hands, look at them.
Do you ask of their emptiness?
You see: they love the land that is not theirs.

Poema a Circe III

Tampoco tú eres mía aunque te amo.
Eres como la tierra, como la isla.
Con nadie te comparto, amor, con nadie.
Yo no puedo decir: aquello es mío.
Esta isla donde amamos no es de nadie.
Lo que se debe a alguien no es de uno.
Y lo prefiero así, porque el amor
Es cual lengua de fuego o universo
Desparramado en vid por todas partes.

La carne es lo ulterior, la brasa misma,
Lo que se busca y ama y estercola.
Fugitiva verdad de luna opaca
En arañazo cruel de zarza ardiendo
Despertando al misterio de las manos,
Al tacto de la boca y a los besos.

Circe, carne eres tú, tierra fecunda
Como la que no tengo en esta isla.
Cierro la palma y el puño y la semilla
Entierro bajo tierra roja y blanda.
Paseamos la tristeza mano a mano.
La carne es un mastín para la sed
Con pámpanos de nata como senos.
Curvo alfanje con filo de cristales
He de abrirme la sed y vaciarme.

Poem to Circe III

You are not mine either even though I love you.
You are like earth, like the island.
I share you with no one, love, no one.
I cannot say: that is mine.
This island where we love belongs to no one.
What is owed doesn't belong to anyone.
I prefer it this way, because love
Is that language of fire or scattered
Universe in vine everywhere.

Flesh is subsequent, the very embers,
What one looks for and loves and composts.
Fleeting truth of an opaque moon
Cruelly scratching the burning bramble,
Awakening to the mystery of hands,
The touch of the mouth and kiss.

Circe, you are flesh, fertile land,
Like the one I don't have on this island.
I close the palm in fist and bury
The seed beneath soft and red earth.
Sadness and I walk hand in hand.
Flesh is thirsty as a mastiff
With vine shoots of cream for breasts.
A crooked swordfish, crystal sharp,
I must open my thirst and empty myself.

Poema a Circe IV

Hemos llegado al mar bronces antiguos.
Falta el hombre que diga: el mar es mío.
Bajo este mar las ánforas fenicias
Duermen su languidez de hembras redondas.
¿Sabes qué son las ánforas, has visto
Qué gravidez la suya y qué elegancia?
Bajo las aguas ríe su blancura
Como un mármol limpísimo, despierta
Su indolencia al amor, se desperezan.
Hace siglos que duermen entre arenas.
Son como peces blandos que escaparan
Al codicioso amor del alfarero.
Son ya del mar lo mismo que marinos
Ahogados en el fondo con las algas.
Marinos extranjeros de países
Lejanos cuyo aroma desvanece.

Con las barbas flotantes y dispersas,
Con las barbas en bucles, extendidas
Como rizos dorados por el mar.
Circe, yo amo las ánforas. Me duele
Verlas fuera del mar, sin mar ni arenas.
Me recuerdan al joven ahogado
Que partió de alborada y se ha dormido
Eternamente azul bajo las aguas.

Poem to Circe IV

Ancient bronzes, we reached the sea.
Missing is the man who says: the sea is mine.
Under this sea Phoenician amphorae
Sleep their languid female curves.
Do you know amphorae? Have you
Seen their figure, their elegance?
Beneath the waters their whiteness
Laughs like spotless marble, indolence
Wakens love, they expand.
They've slept between sands for centuries.
They are like soft fish that escaped
The potter's greedy love.
They already belong to the sea much as
Drowned sailors at the bottom of the algae.
Foreign sailors from faraway
Countries whose fragrance dissipates.

With floating and dispersed beards,
With beards in loops, extended
By the sea like golden curls.
Circe, I love amphorae. It hurts me
To see them out of the sea, without sea or sand.
They remind me of the drowned youth
Who left at dawn and has forever been
sleeping blue beneath the waters.

Poema a Circe IX

Iluminado soy humanamente.
Me sorprendo a diario con el canto
Que ruge y se desborda como un jugo
Erosivo de moras, con el canto
Alegre y tumultuoso de los hombres.
Se distienden las voces como pámpanos,
Las huellas como pámpanos, la carne
Semejante a mi carne, y es el viento
Jugoso de la vida el que madura.
Reencarno con sus huellas de hace siglos,
Sus voces seculares, su alegría
Tantas veces penosa, como el hijo
Enfermo que se lleva a las espaldas.
Es en esta isla, Circe, donde siento
La fuerza de vivir extrañamente.
Aquí la humanidad se abraza y grita
Mezclando con la risa sus colores,
Hablando el mismo idioma con acentos
Variados. La evidencia del amor
Se transforma en un rito que oficiamos.

Llegamos y el milagro se produjo.
Ha sido el mar y el viento en las campanas.
Veníamos de lejos, de los años
Sedientos como polvo, de las redes
De humildes pescadores en mar yerma.
Llegamos y el milagro con nosotros.
Ha saltado a la red como un pez líquido
Y se ha multiplicado para todos
Y nos hemos saciado, y todos, todos
Andamos por la arena como un solo.
Ya ves, Circe, el milagro se produce
Siempre que el hombre lo quiere. La búsqueda
He ahí el misterio de todas las cosas.

Poem to Circe IX

Humanly I'm illuminated.
I'm amazed every day by the roaring
Song that overflows like erosive
Blackberry juice, by the joyful
And boisterous song of men.
Voices stretch like branches,
Footprints like branches, flesh
Kindred to my flesh, and life's
Juicy wind ripens.
I reincarnate with their centuries old footprints,
Their secular voices, their joy
So often painful, like a sick
Child carried on one's back.
Oddly it's on this island, Circe,
I have the strength to live.
Here humanity is embraced and screams
Mixing laughter with its colors,
Speaking the same language with varied
Accents. Love's display
Becomes a ritual we officiate.

We arrived and the miracle happened.
It was the sea and the wind in the bells.
We came from far, from years
Thirsty as dust, from humble
fishermen's nets on barren shore.
We arrived and the miracle with us.
It jumped into the net like liquid fish
And multiplied for all
And we satiated ourselves, and all of us
We all walk through the sand as one.
You see, Circe, the miracle occurs
Whenever man wants it. The search
That is the mystery of all things.

Poema a Circe XII

Entonces te soñaba a mi manera.
La distancia es un poltro que cabalga
En sentido contrario a rienda suelta.
Te soñaba y te hacía a mi medida.
Fuí yo quien te creé, no como eres.
Porque el barro se escapa y eres huella
Escapada al amor del alfarero,
Sino como el amor te iba haciendo.
Te he creado, Circe; humanamente
He ido recreándome en tu imágen,
He ido recreándote y viviendo
Mi creación en tí, hasta ignorar
O confundir, a fuerza de saber,
Dónde empezabas tú, realidad,
Y dónde terminaba yo, deseo.

Alta eras en mis sueños,
Inaccesible casi como una isla
Que se busca y se busca durante años.
Te veía en los Picos de la Sierra,
En la nieve lilial de la montaña
Emerger de mis sueños como águila.
Como águila quedabas fijamente
Mirando al sol, abierto tu plumaje
Negrísimo y alado mensajero.
Te hice así de mi carne. La saliva
Se mojaba en tu polvo enfebrecido
Y te iba recreando a imagen mía.

Alta me abriste herida dolorosa
Lanceando la piel hasta encontrarte
Creada corazón en mi costado.
Era el tiempo un olivo como aquellos
Del cáliz y la entrega. Yo era el hombre
Que atiende al sacrificio. Era la espera.
Todo se ha consumado, Circe, y vivo.

Poem to Circe XII

Then I dreamt of you in my way.
Distance is a colt galloping
In the opposite direction at full speed.
I dreamt you and made you in my size.
I'm the one who created you, but not how you are.
Because mud escapes and you are a trace
Broken free from the potter's love
Except love itself was making you.
I created you, Circe; humanly
I keep recreating me in your image,
I keep recreating you and living
My creation in you, until I don't know
Or confuse, by dint of knowing,
Where you, reality, start
And where I, desire, end.

Exalted were you in my dreams,
Almost inaccessible like an island
Sought and sought for years.
I saw you in the Sierra Peaks,
In the lilial mountain snow
Emerge like an eagle from my dreams.
Like an eagle you stared
At the sun, your jet black plumage
Open winged, messenger.
I made you thus of my flesh. Saliva
Soaked in your feverish dust,
I kept recreating you in my image.

Exalted you opened my painful wound
Lancing the skin until you found yourself,
Heart, created in my side.
Time was an olive tree like those
Of the chalice and surrender. I was the man
Attending to the sacrifice. I was the wait.
All is consumed, Circe, and I live.

Poema a Circe XV

¿Por qué ansiosos caminos de derrota
Has llegado a tu orilla? ¿Por qué andinas
Soledades en calma permanezco
Como herbolario ecuestre de tus lomas?
La caverna es el templo y sus columnas,
Donde el jaspe humedece las culebras,
Han desbordado el rapto de la esfinge.
Nunca sabremos qué fueron las crines.
Hubo siempre preguntas en las llagas,
Preguntas escapadas al silencio.
Pero el canto sutil no ha sido dicho.
He guardado el secreto de las voces,
Ariadna, digo Circe, digo isla,
Cósmicamente hablando y contradigo,
He afirmado bastante, la aventura
Encadenado al mástil por los otros.

No quise nunca cerrar los oídos.
Aunque el maceramiento se cebara
En mis uñas y fuera como azogue
Aquella voz, aquellas voces raras
Que no oyeron los otros por su miedo.
Y la metamorfosis y el hechizo,
¿Hasta qué punto son indisolubles?
Digo el amor, la ira no el regreso
Cuando estaba en camino y se cambiaba
Esa vuelta en un templo ilimitado.
No entiendo la abundancia ni las lluvias,
Pero creo que somos de lo mismo,
Que es oficio de reyes destronados
Y con poco sostengo mi vigilia.
No me preguntes más por la medida
De mis brazos prudentes. La distancia
Cuenta a veces tan poco como el tiempo.

Poem to Circe XV

By what uneasy paths of defeat
Did you reach your shore? By what Andean
Loneliness do I remain serene
Like the equestrian herbalist of your knolls?
The cave is the temple and its columns —
Where jasper dampens the snakes —
Have flooded the rapture of the Sphinx.
We will never know what happened to the mane.
There were always questions in the wounds,
Questions broken loose from silence.
But the subtle song hasn't been told.
I kept the secret of the voices,
Ariadne, I say Circe, I say island,
Speaking cosmically, and I dare —
I have declared enough — the adventure,
Chained to the mast by others.

I never wanted to close my ears.
Even though mortification devoured
My nails and that voice was like
Quicksilver, those strange voices
Others didn't hear for fear.
And metamorphosis and spell,
To what extent are they inseparable?
I say love, I say anger, not to return
When I set forth and this homeward
Journey turned into a boundless temple.
I don't understand abundance and rainfall
But believe our essence the same,
Which is the trade of dethroned kings.
And with little I hold my vigil.
Don't ask me anymore about the extent
Of my watchful arms. Distance
Counts sometimes as little as time.

Poema a Circe XVII

Y permanezco solo y extrañado.
El prodigio se anuncia en la garganta
De los hombres que sufren. Tempestades
Han cubierto las gradas de mi templo
Con hormigas vivientes, y el despojo
Permanece en la orilla como un cuerpo
Desnudo. Han descendido porteadores
Con sus cánticos negros y el aroma
De las voces ardía como incienso.
Sus manos he apretado una por una,
Eran manos abiertas y rugosas.
Manos ásperas de hombres implacables.
No explicaré el clamor de los tambores,
El clamor de la selva cuando pasa
El caminante ciego entre los tilos
Y el silencio se extiende y nunca acaba.

Circe, tú reconoces, tú descifras
El color del augurio y los enigmas.
Yo espero siempre la revelación.
Yo soy de los que creen en la magia.
Yo quiero ver la máscara y la pulpa.
Yo araño la corteza y muerdo el tallo.
Yo te he creado, Circe, y no te ignoro.
Mis tambores te siguen por la selva.
He arrancado los ojos de millares
De esclavos para que velen tus pasos.
He cortado las manos que más amo
Y las llevas contigo y te preservan
De otras manos azules y curvadas.
He dejado sin pies a mis amigos
Para que andes mejor en el desierto.

Poem to Circe XVII

And I remain alone and amazed.
The wonder is announced in the throat
Of men who suffer. Storms
Have covered the steps of my temple
With anthills, and the rubble
Remains on the shore like a naked
Body. Porters have descended
With their black canticles and the aroma
Of the voices burned like incense.
I clasped their hands one by one,
They were open and rugged hands.
Coarse hands of relentless men.
I will not explain the clamor of drums,
The clamor of the jungle when the blind
Traveler passes between the lindens
And the silence spreads out and never ends.

Circe, you recognize, you decipher
Enigmas and the color of the omen.
I always await the revelation.
I am among those who believe in magic.
I want to see the mask and pulp.
I scratch the bark and bite the stem.
I created you, Circe, and I don't ignore you.
My drums follow you through the forest.
I ripped the eyes of thousands
Of slaves to ensure your steps.
I cut the hands I love most
And you take them with you and they protect
You from other blue and curved hands.
I have left my friends without feet
So you can walk better through the desert.

Hay un coro de voces que repiten
Tu nombre con sus voces cercenadas.
He sembrado de ídolos la jungla
Y he quemado las tribus y la hoguera
Ascendía en el bronce, perpetuaba
Con su fuego clamante tu figura.
He mordido los sexos de mujeres
Como columnas y el espamo
Se cebaba en tu imagen, se cebaba
Hasta estallar la carne y mutilarse.

Hay garras de leones con la sangre
Aún fresca de sus víctimas que graban
Tu nombre sobre mármol y custodia
Tu efigie entre sus zarpas homicidas.

Yo sigo en la isla que azotan tifones
Encadenados al mar cuando las olas
Se abaten contra el dique, y te pregono.
Grito, hasta enronquecer, tu nombre amado.

There is a chorus of voices repeating
Your name with their severed voices.
I have sown the jungle with idols
And burned the tribes and the bonfire
Rose in bronze, perpetuating
Your figure with its ardent clamor.
I have bitten the sexes of women
Like columns and the spasm
Raged in your image, it raged
Until the flesh exploded, mutilating itself.

Lion claws — their victims'
Blood still fresh — engrave
Your name in marble and guard
Your effigy in their murderous paws.

I carry on in this island whipped by typhoons
Chained to the sea when the waves
Crash against the dam, and I proclaim you.
I scream, until hoarse, your beloved name.

Poema a Circe XVIII

Voy a dejar atrás el promontorio.
Al que pregunte responderé: *Nadie*.
No tiene techo mi alcoba, no hay vigas
Que sostengan los muros, ni ornamentos.
El navegante ignora las paredes,
No conozco ni patria ni la busco.
No pertenezco a nadie y abandono
El hogar que no es mío, las cosechas.
Los frutos y las cosas que se cambian
Los hombres entre sí, que se reparten
Como botín de guerra los gigantes.
Los poderosos dicen que son suyas.
Todo está repartido, todo es de alguien.

No pertenezco a raza de gigantes.
No quiero tomar nada entre mis manos.
Abomino del látigo y la espuela,
Del todopoderoso que reparte
La miseria y el hambre a manos llenas.
No me he sentado nunca entre tiranos,
Pero me sentaría con ladrones
Antes y besaría a los leprosos
Y sería feliz con sus mujeres.

Yo soy de los que mueren en suplicio.
Tú reconoces, Circe, mi sandalias
Cuando vuelvo cansado; reconoces
Mi rostro entre millares, mi sonrisa.
Besas la mano que estrecha las manos
De los desheredados y sonríes.
Si preguntan qué nombre tengo, *Nadie*,
Responderé. Me llamo Nadie, Nadie,
Y no poseo nada, y no me duele
Porque así puedo andar con menos peso.

Poem to Circe XVIII

I'm going to leave behind the promontory.
When they ask I will answer: *No one*.
My bedroom has no roof, no beams
holding up the walls, no ornaments.
The navigator ignores walls,
I know of no country nor seek any.
I belong to no one and leave
the home that is not mine, the crops,
fruits and things that men
exchange, that giants
distribute as spoils of war.
The powerful say they are theirs.
All is divided, everything belongs to someone.

I don't belong to a race of giants.
I don't want to take anything in my hands.
I abhor the whip and spur,
the almighty who dispenses
poverty and hunger hand over fist.
I never sat between tyrants
but would sit with thieves
first and kiss the lepers
and be happy with their wives.

I am of those dying in agony.
Circe, you recognize my sandals
when I come back tired; you recognize
my face among thousands, my smile.
You kiss the hand that shakes hands
with the disowned and you smile.
If they ask me what is my name, I will
answer, *No one*. My name is No one, No one,
and I own nothing, and it doesn't hurt me
because this way I walk with less weight.

Poema a Circe XIX

No vengo a poner orden en las cosas,
Ni estaré mucho tiempo entre vosotros.
El extranjero sabe que no es suya
La tierra que más ama y permanece
Como un marino extraño entre los hombres.
Cuando llegue el momento de partir,
Cuando el viento levante sus amarras,
Y las jarcias se envuelvan con el humo
Misterioso del alba y sea blando
El limo de los peces y la gruta
Donde sacrificamos a los dioses,
Cuando no me veáis entre vosotros,
Abandonad al olvido mi nombre.
No os dejo nada y no llevo conmigo
Nada. No quedan anclas ni estandartes
Para conmemorar mi permanencia.

Sólo el cuchillo largo de los astros
En los ojos abiertos de la noche.
No he venido a pedir, ni a dar, ni a ser.
No he venido a sembrar en vuestros campos
Ni pienso recoger para el invierno.
He estado con vosotros, eso es todo.
Circe sabe qué astros, qué tormentas,
Qué lunas de milenio me han traído.
Yo conozco los signos que presiden
El exilio y la muerte y me abandono
A una sangre color de miel oscura.

Yo soy iconoclasta y rompo ídolos.
Yo afirmo y niego con la misma fuerza.
Los que me conocéis sabéis qué fuego
Hay en mis decisiones, qué barbarie
Acompaña mi risa, qué locura
Ha mordido mi pecho y cómo ladran
Sobre mi corazón negros mastines.

Poem to Circe XIX

I did not come to put things in order,
Nor will I spend much time among you.
The foreigner knows that the land
He most loves is not his and he remains
Like an unfamiliar sailor among men.
When it's time to leave,
When the wind raises its moorings
And the rigging is wrapped with the mysterious
Smoke of dawn and the fish
Slime is soft in the grotto
Where we sacrifice to the gods,
When you do not see me among you,
Abandon my name to oblivion.
I leave you nothing and I take nothing
With me. There are no anchors or banners
To commemorate my tenure.

Only the long knife of the stars
In the night's open eyes.
I haven't come to ask, or to give, or to be.
I haven't come to sow in your fields
Nor do I think of collecting for winter.
I have been with you, that's all.
Circe knows what stars, what storms,
What millennial moons brought me.
I know the signs ruling exile
And death and abandon myself
To a dark honey blood.

I am iconoclastic and break idols.
I affirm and deny with the same force.
Those who know me know the fire
In my decisions, what brutal force
Accompanies my laughter, what madness
Has bitten my chest and the black
Mastiffs barking on my heart.

—Ha sido sólo un hombre que se supo
Hombre por dentro y fuera. Un extranjero
Que arribó, vió y amó. Ciudadano
De la isla los humildes lo adoptaron.
Un hombre encuadernado con piel de hombre.

—Y vive todavía y os recuerda.

—It was just a man who knew himself
A man inside and out. A stranger
Who arrived, saw and loved. The humble
Adopted him a citizen of the island.
A man bound with human skin.

—And he is still alive and remembers you.

Poema a Circe XX

Inmortal para el dolor, agobiado
Por el peso doliente de la especie,
Bajo el árbol crecido de la carne
Presiento mi corona como un yugo
Macerado de hierros y cristales.
No en vano la condena me acompaña
Y yo he cargado a espaldas el madero
Espumoso de sangre y violáceo.
Tengo la fuerza eral de los volcanes
Y alimento mi sed con la aventura.
Ya reconoces, Circe, mi osamenta.
Ya ves cómo se anuncia el cataclismo.
Ya sabes cómo huelen mis andrajos
Y el color de la herida que se oculta
Cuando brillan de frente dos cuchillos.
Circe, la encarnación vive conmigo.

Encarno en cada hombre, en cada resto
De hombre atormentado, en cada scoria
De hombre envilecido, en cada grito
De hombre ajusticiado, en cada esputo
Y juramento roto y voz clamante
De hombre despojado y sojuzgado.
Circe, yo amo la carne. Tú conoces,
Y lo conoces todo, nada escapa
A tu mirada astral de esfinge ciega,
Qué soga de lujuria me aprisiona,
Yo amo los miembros desnudos, yo muerdo
La herida miel de sexos como escarcha.
Yo proclamo mi negra taumaturgia.
Más arriba que dios, en las tinieblas
Del muérdago y la carne, tiemblo y clamo.
He venido a romper corona y yugo,
A rebelar mendigos y liberar esclavos.
He cambiado mi paz por el cuchillo.
Estoy aquí para abolizar la Muerte.
Los que creáis en mi no moriréis.
Yo amo el dolor: mi Reino es de este mundo.

Poem to Circe XX

Immortal for pain, burdened
by the heavy suffering of the species,
Under the tree grown from flesh
I presage my crown like a yoke
Macerated in irons and crystals.
Verdict is not my companion in vain
And I've carried on my back the tree
Foaming purple blood.
I have the ageless power of volcanoes
And I feed my thirst for adventure.
You already recognize, Circe, my bones.
You already see how the cataclysm is announced.
You already know how my rags smell
And the color of the wound that is hidden
When two knives shine ahead.
Circe, incarnation lives with me.

I embody each man, each remnant
Of tormented man, each slag
Of debased man, each cry
Of executed man, each spit
And broken oath and clamorous voice
Of despoiled and subdued man.
Circe, I love the flesh. You know,
And you know everything, nothing escapes
Your astral gaze of blind sphinx.
What noose of lust imprisons me,
I love the naked members, I bite
The honey wound of sexes like icing.
I proclaim my black thaumaturgy.
Higher than God, in the darkness
Of mistletoe and flesh, I tremble and clamor.
I've come to break crown and yoke,
Rebel beggars and free slaves.
I traded my peace for the knife.
I'm here to abolish Death.
Those who believe in me will not die.
I love the pain: my Kingdom is of this world.

II
El Vendimiador

II
The Vintner

Ibiza

Os voy a decir un nombre como escrito en la cal
por el índice de fuego de un arcángel selvático.
Hay nombres que son el fuego,
como cortados a pico.
Este es el nombre que llevo en las rayas de mis manos,
el nombre que dice una leyenda
y escribe la historia de mis veinticinco años.

Es hermoso nacer como los pájaros
sobre un nido de piedra,
alzar las alas como una antena de luz
sobre la mar amarga,
llevar en las alas escrito
el nombre de la amada.
Pero más hermoso todavía
es ser esta ave rara, esta espada silente
como una lengua de ofidio,
esa hoguera encendida de lava y rocas,
ese nombre alargado en los arroyos,
ese cuerpo esperado en la canícula,
esa voz, esas manos, esa boca,
ese arañazo íntimo de fábulas o cristales.
He aquí por qué soy como soy,
por qué me llamo de esta manera y no de otra,
por qué la tierra me ha hecho prisionero.
Este es el misterio,
un nombre, una palabra, una hoguera,
un poco de geografía.

Estoy atenazado por amor
entre cuatro paredes de cal viva.
Bajo los limoneros,
a la sombra olorosa de los granados,
donde huelen la albahaca y los romeros,
del talle de palmeras como hermosas mujeres.

Ibiza

I will tell you a name as written in lime
by the fiery index finger of a sylvan archangel.
There are names that are the fire
as if roughly sewn.
This is the name I bear in the lines of my hands,
the name that tells a legend
and writes the story of my twenty five years.

It is beautiful to be born like birds
on a stone nest,
lift the wings like an antenna of light
over the bitter sea,
carry the name of the beloved
on the wings.
But more beautiful still
is to be this rare bird, this sword silent
like a snake tongue,
this blaze of burning lava and rocks,
this name stretched in the brooks,
this body awaited in the midsummer heat,
this voice, these hands, this mouth,
this innermost scratch of fable and glass.
This is why I am the way I am,
why I am named this way and no other,
why the land has made me prisoner.
This is the mystery,
a name, a word, a blaze,
a little geography.

I am crushed by love
between four walls of live lime.
Under the lemon trees,
in the scented shade of pomegranate trees,
where basil and rosemary exude their aromas,
the figure of palm trees as if beautiful women.

Ya sabéis el misterio de mi vida,
ese nombre de laca que os descubre
la sed mis salinas.
Ya sabéis ese nombre de tortura,
ese nombre de higuera y de membrillo,
ese oloroso ramo de azahares,
ese velo espumoso de mar embravecida
donde anidan las aves,
esa mujer lasciva de cabellera roja
que ha escrito la leyenda de mis veinticinco años.

Ya no tengo misterio a vuestros ojos.
Soy el hombre de la isla de Ibiza.

Now you know the mystery of my life,
this lacquer name unearthed for you
by the thirst of my salt works.
Now you know this name of torture,
this name of fig tree and quince,
this fragrant branch of orange blossoms,
this frothy shroud of rough sea
where the birds nest,
this lustful woman with red mane
who wrote the legend of my twenty five years.

Now I have no mystery for you.
I am the man from the island of Ibiza.

Oda a un joven marino

A mi hermano Manuel

El mar es una novia con los brazos abiertos,
con los pechos macizos como balas de goma.
Es difícil negarse a su caricia,
secarse de los labios su regusto salobre,
olvidar su amargor azucarado.
Bajo sus aguas gime un rosario de muertos
centauros veladores de las sombras.
Hombres hermosos, duros, como anclas arrancadas
del pecho de un dios bárbaro.

Es difícil negarse a la llamada
del mar, taparse los oídos,
agarrar con las dos manos el cuello
y enmudecer de súbito, o arrancarse los ojos
y darlos a los peces. Ignorar las gaviotas
y los mástiles rojos y tantas banderolas,
y los barcos que llegan de países ignotos
y los barcos que parten para otros países
que apenas se conocen, o quizá para el nuestro.

Porque nosotros llevamos adentro
como una quilla azul o arboladura
el amargor marino de las algas,
las barras sobre el dorso de los peces,
la muerte alquitranada
y nuestras iniciales escritas en el mar.

La mar de los marinos, vuestra novia
hermano que te alejas sobre el Puente
como un pedazo más de nuestra isla.
Tú sabes el olor que huele a la muerte
porque pisas debajo un cementerio
que puede ser el tuyo y vas alegre.

Ode to a Young Mariner

To my brother Manuel

The sea is a bride with open arms,
with stout rubber balls for breasts.
It is difficult to refuse her caress,
dry from the lips her brackish aftertaste,
forget her sweet bitterness.
Underneath her waters wails a rosary of dead
centaurs, watchmen of the shadows.
Handsome men, hard as anchors torn
from the chest of a barbarian god.

It is difficult to refuse the call
of the sea, cover one's ears,
grasp the neck with both hands
and become suddenly mute, or pluck out one's eyes
and feed them to the fish. To ignore the gulls
and red masts and so many pennants,
and the ships arriving from unknown countries
and the ships departing for others
barely known, or perhaps for ours.

Because we carry within
like a blue keel or masts and spars
the marine bitterness of kelp,
the stripes on the back of fishes,
the tarry death
and our initials written in the sea.

The sea of mariners, your bride,
brother moving away to the Bridge
like one more piece of our island.
You know the smell of death
because you tread beneath a cemetery
that can be yours and you go brightly.

Tú sabes como huele el mar a vida,
como vomita a veces fiera espuma,
como salvaje gime y se rebela
igual que un ser atávico, criatura primitiva.

Llevamos todos dentro la muerte escrita a surcos
como un nombre trazado por la quilla
de tu barco en el mar. Somos todos marinos
de una novia dormida con los pechos redondos.

Yo no quiero partir para la tierra,
brotar como una rama de eucalipto
con los ojos cegados por la hierba.
Espérame tú, hermano, cuando ancles tu nave
en la mar que has amado.
No has de partir tan solo, marinero
hermano de un marino atenazado
por las fauces abiertas de la tierra.

You know how the sea smells of life,
how at times she spits a ferocious foam,
how she wails wild and rises
like an atavistic being, a primitive creature.

We all carry death within written in furrows
like a name traced by the keel
of your boat in the sea. We are all sailors
of a sleeping bride with round breasts.

I don't want to depart for the land,
to sprout like a eucalyptus branch
my eyes blinded by grass.
Wait for me, brother, when you anchor
your vessel in the sea you've loved.
No need to depart so alone, mariner
brother of a seaman gripped
by the earth's open jaws.

Tom Smithson
muerto en su buhardilla

A Carlos Germán Belli

Te has ido
por las espirales de humo de tus dedos
        famélicos.
Te has alzado sobre la marea encendida de
        Long Island
quizá para soñar mejor desde el fondo de tus
        párpados ecuestres
en aquellos manjares que tu paladar de clown
        hambriento
no llegó sino a intuir.
Es falso decir que te has muerto,
que te han vomitado para siempre como una
        cosa inútil.
Tu sueño debe ser tan leve como el plumaje
        de las prostitutas de California
tan grácil como uno de esos ascensores de
        Manhattan.
Temen verte despertar a deshora
para ir hacia Wall Street y decir a los
        fabricantes de embutidos
que es hermoso dictar cartas comerciales a
        las rubias mecanógrafas,
pero más hermoso vagar por las riberas del
        Hudson.
Como aquel día de enero,
aquel amanecer de labios jóvenes y pechos
        transparentes
cuando dirigiste tus sueños al escaparate de
        dulces,
tan asombrado,
tan hondamente sorprendido de hallar a Dios
        entre las tartas de crema

Tom Smithson
Dead in his Garret

to Carlos Germán Belli

You left
through the smoke spirals of your famished
      fingers.
You arose above the burning tide
      of Long Island
perhaps to better dream from the depth of your
      equestrian eyelids
of tasty morsels that your hungry clown
      palate
could only imagine.
It is false to say you died,
that they vomited you forever as if
      a useless thing.
Your sleep must be as light as the plumage
      of the California whores
as graceful as one of those Manhattan
      elevators.
They fear seeing you wake at some unearthly hour
to go toward Wall Street and tell
      the sausage makers
that it is beautiful to dictate commercial letters
      to the blond typists,
but even more beautiful to wander the banks
      of the Hudson.
Like that January day,
that sunrise of young lips and sheer
      breasts
when you directed your dreams
      toward the pastry shop,
so astonished,
so deeply surprised to discover God
      amidst the cream tarts

y sentir su peso sobre las lívidas paredes de
      tu estómago.
Ya sólo queda un revuelo de cenizas, y tu
      nombre
voceado por el muchacho de los periódicos.

and feel his weight on your stomach's
           livid walls.
Now only a flutter of ashes remains, and your
           name
voiced by the newspaper boy.

El hombre y la piedra

Aquí estoy de regreso. Encadenado
por una soledad que es como un vino.
Con el puño en el puño, y el camino
errante y atrozmente equivocado.

Con la piel del revés, el gesto alzado.
El hombre soy y juego mi destino.
He de perder más no me importa el tino
si rompo el yugo que me oprime airado.

Arrastro y pongo en juego mi alegría.
Mi carcajada triste, mi condena
sopesada en el fiel de cada día.

Hombre de barro sucio y patena,
hombre de limo y cal. De idolatría.
Como un coloso con los pies de arena.

The Man and the Stone

Here I have returned. Chained
by a wine like solitude.
Fist in fist, and the way
nomadic and atrociously astray.

With the skin inside out, the face up thrown,
I am the man and play my destiny.
I have more to lose and don't care for rhyme or reason
if I break the violent yoke oppressing me.

I trail and throw in my elation,
my sad laughter, my condemnation
weighed in every day admonition.

Man of paten and of mud dirty,
Man of silt and lime. Of idolatry.
Like a colossus with clay feet.

III
Otros Poemas

III
Other Poems

Desde el Ponto Euxino

And I said: Tomorrow I will lie on the South side.

— Ezra Pound

A Juan Bernier, amigo y maestro,
desde este destierro mío y con la esperanza
de regresar un día a mi Celeste Córdoba enjuta.

El viajero

Inhóspita ciudad. Encanecidos
viajeros solitarios la mirada
hemos dejado atrás.
Fue Itaca y en Itaca la inclemencia
de amaneceres lentos como lluvia
que todo lo fecunda y nada engendra.

El augurio latía en nuestras sienes
la palabra profética ascendía
y se alejaban las naves y al conjuro
de signos cercenados
nuestros pasos guiaba
alejándose
germinando en los sueños
más allá de los arcos y los templos
incendiando los mástiles
con gritos o presagios o señales
que apenas se sabrían y más nunca
se volvieron a oir.

Inhóspita ciudad. Sombras sólo
habríamos sido. Eriales.
Y el sueño cubrirá
la tierra de nieve y olvido.

From the Euxine Sea

And I said: Tomorrow I will lie on the South side.

— Ezra Pound

To Juan Bernier, friend and mentor,
from this exile of mine and with the hope
to return one day to my spare Celestial Córdoba.

The Traveler

Inhospitable city. Grizzled
solitary travelers, we left
our sight behind.
It was Ithaca and in Ithaca the inclemency
of slow sunrises like rain
that impregnates all and breeds nothing.

The oracle throbbed on our temples,
the prophetic word rose
and the ships receded and under the spell
of subdued signs
it guided our steps
receding
sprouting in our dreams
beyond the archways and temples
inflaming the masts
with bellows or portents or signs
that would be hardly known and never
to be heard again.

Inhospitable city.
We were only shadows. Unplowed.
And the dream will cloak
the earth with snow and oblivion.

No habrá regreso nunca.
¿Por qué habremos querido siempre avanzar
adentrarnos en selvas
abrazarnos al vértigo?

Fue a veces el jazmín y otras la rosa
y los campos de jara y cantueso
y a veces los jacintos la retama
y otras veces el lirio.
Inhóspita ciudad. Enamorado
mar sin otro horizonte y estandarte
que el resto de naufragios palpitando
como una luz de antorchas.

La huella

Y a tus pies no hollarán las ruinas de Tebas
ni habrá ciudad doliente ni tampoco
resucitados cuerpos que conjuren
soledad y dolor.

Perdidos recobrados nuestros huesos
sudarios ceniciento arboladura
los festejos dirán de antiguos días.

Aquel que estaba muerto vivo yace
en la tierra remota
y no hay bronces que doblen
cuando el añil del alba es su regazo.

Yaces en tierra porque el mar
ha devuelto los huesos uno a uno
ha devuelto la carne sepultada
ha devuelto el cadáver que retoña
erguido entre los cedros.

There will be no return ever.
Why the will to always move forward
to go deeper into forests
and embrace the maelstrom?

It was at times the jasmine, then the rose
and the fields of rockrose and lavender
at times the hyacinths, the broom
and at others the iris.
Inhospitable city. Seafaring
love with no other horizon or banner
than the debris of shipwrecks fluttering
like a torchlight.

The track

No longer will your feet tread the ruins of Thebes
there will be no grieving city nor
resurrected bodies to ward off
solitude and pain.

Our lost bones recovered
shafts of ashen shrouds
the feasts will speak of ancient times.

The living dead lies
in the far land
and no bell will toll
when the indigo dawn is his refuge.

You lie inland because the sea
brought back the bones one by one
brought back the buried flesh
brought back the corpse that sprouts
raised amidst the cedars.

El oráculo

Habíamos tomado asiento
junto a la Esfinge a solas
en el acantilado. Recordamos
el naufragio de entonces
tiempo alado
de caricias y sones de trompeta
el delirio sin freno de alboradas
que nunca volverán
pasos perdidos
en la nieve y el sueño.

Inhóspita ciudad.
Memoria intacta
de almenas abrasadas
hoy ceniza
resplandores de incendio
y el aullido
del can que en nuestra marcha
quedaría hierático en la orilla
sacrificio supremo
o agonía de un orbe que bosteza.

The oracle

We had taken a seat
next to the Sphinx alone
on the cliff. We evoked
the shipwreck of those days
time winged
with caresses and trumpet sounds
the unbridled frenzy of dawns
that will never recur
lost footprints
in the snow and sleep.

Inhospitable city.
Intact memory
of merlons ablaze
now ashes
incandescent combustion
and the howl
of the hound that in our procession
would remain petrified on the shore
ultimate sacrifice
or agony of a yawning world.

Cimetière de Montrouge

Uno hay que descansa en los vivos
su muerte de ciprés resucitada.
Germina el trigo en sus manos de hierba
porque a manos y a trigos
se volvó.
César de trueno y rabia,
pregonero
hermoso de la paz.
Yo revivo tu rostro de pan quemado,
puño sin hiel abierto a la esperanza.
Sobre la torre Eiffel
percibo tu osamenta de dios encadenado,
tu arquitectura ronca
de hombre de pan, of César y Vallejo.

París, 1955

Montrouge Cemetery

There is one who among the living rests,
his death resuscitated by cypresses.
The wheat sprouts in his hand of grasses
because to wheat and hands
he fell.
César of rage and thunder,
town crier
for peace nonpareil.
I relive your bread burnt face,
unscathed fist open to faith.
Over the Eiffel tower
I perceive your chained god bones,
your raucous architecture
of the man of bread, of César y Vallejo.

Paris, 1955

El embeleso

For worse? for better? but happened.
— Ezra Pound

A Mariano Villangómez,
con una nostalgia inmensa

Puede que las cosas no sean
como quisiéramos que fuesen.

El río sigue su curso
y lo contemplamos atónitos.

Este río será el mismo que vieran
los ojos de Heráclito aunque no sea
el mismo río.
Cavilo así, embelesado
a orillas del Danubio
esta tarde otoñal
en que fluyen las aguas, sarmentosas,
como ramificadas, arrastrando
vestigios de tormenta, ranúnculos,
despojos ribereños de un paisaje
que sí sería el mismo hace mil años.
Sólo el hombre es capaz de destruir
lo que nunca ha creado
y que él sólo cree pertenecerle.
Ver para vivir no le basta,
todo tiene que ser suyo, apropiárselo.

No pienso que nunca salgamos
de la caverna. Lobo, tigre y buitre,
vocablos que el hombre ha inventado
huyendo de sí mismo,
cercenando ese doble ingrato
que refleja el espejo al contemplarse

The Spell

For worse? for better? but happened.
— Ezra Pound

*A Mariano Villangómez,
with immense nostalgia*

It's possible things are not
as we wish them to be.

The river follows its course
and we watch it astonished.

This is the same river witnessed
by Heraclitus' eyes even though it's not
the same river.
I ponder this way, spellbound
on the banks of the Danube
this fall afternoon
when the waters flow, furrowed,
as if ramified, dragging
vestiges of storm, ranunculi,
riverside spoils of a landscape
that would be the same a thousand years ago.
Only man is capable of destroying
what he never created
and he alone believes belongs to him.
Seeing is not enough to live,
everything has to be his, owned.

I don't think we'll ever leave
the cave. Wolf, tiger and vulture,
words man invented
fleeing from himself,
clipping this doubly ungrateful person
reflected by the mirror he contemplates

en él, nada tienen que ver
con la naturaleza.
Y, a irlos suprimiendo,
borrándolos de su vida, el espejo
se los devuelve intactos,
convertidos en monstruos, encarnados
en su especie, y serán
ese homo sapiens del que hablan los libros.
Pesadillas horribles nos asaltan
y al despertar nos gustaría
seguir soñando por no ver los cuerpos
de tanto supliciado.
En todas las edades, sublimando
sus propios horrores, el hombre
crea los dioses a su semejanza
y sacrificándolos,
se engañará creyendo redimirse.

Se extinguirá la especie humana
sin haber alcanzado nunca
la edad de la razón, como esas muelas
que se dicen ser las del juicio, tardías,
dolorosas e inútiles, vestigio
como el hombre de otras edades.
Perecerá también
ese embeleso que me habita
a orillas del Danubio y al perderme
por los campos de Córdoba
que dieron su caballo al romancero
o al evocar al Júcar
y las hoces del Huécar
y al bañarme en las fuentes siempre heladas
del río Cuervo y subir a la Vega
del Codorno,
o cuando en Delfos, tras el crepúsculo

himself in, they have nothing
to do with nature.
And, as he eliminates them,
erasing them from his life, the mirror
returns them to him intact,
transformed into monsters, embodied
in his species, and they must be
this homo sapiens the books talk about.
Horrible nightmares assail us
and upon waking we would like
to keep dreaming so as not to see the bodies
of so many tormented souls.
In all ages, as he exalts
his own horrors, man
creates gods in his likeness
and by sacrificing them
fools himself believing he is redeemed.

The human species will die out
without ever reaching
the age of reason, like those teeth
called wisdom, tardy,
painful and useless, vestige
like man of other times.
This spell that inhabits me on the banks
of the Danube will perish too
and as I lose myself
past the fields of Córdoba
famed for ballads
or as I evoke the Júcar
and the Huécar's gorge
and as I bathe in the always icy springs
of the river Cuervo and go up
the Vega del Codorno,
or when in Delphi, after a splendid

de un día esplenderoso, me detengo
entre los olivares plateados
y corono mis sienes
con el laurel de Apolo
y evoco, emplazo a mis antepasados
fundido como acuñado en el mármol
de una tierra que pudo ser la mía
y de la que surgió una vez
la única raza humana que valía
la pena así llamarse.

Aquí y ahora siento en mí crecer
y que de mí dimana
como un aura celeste, límpida,
etérea, grandiosa,
y recuerdo a Cernuda, el hermano
y guía memorable,
y recuerdo con él que el hombre,
sólo el hombre que él y yo sabemos,
siempre quiso caer
donde el amor fue suyo un día.

Viena, 31 de agosto de 1995

day's sunset, I linger
amidst silvery olive groves
and crown my temples
with Apollo's laurel
and evoke, summon my ancestors,
cast as if minted in the marble
of a land that could have been mine
and from which once emerged
the only human race
worth that name.

Here and now I feel grow in me
and arise from me
a kind of celestial aura, limpid,
ethereal, grandiose,
and I remember Cernuda, illustrious
brother and guide,
and I reminisce with him that mankind,
the mankind he and I know,
always wanted to fall
where love once belonged.

Vienna, 31 August 1995

CUATRO SONETOS ÓRFICOS

FOUR ORPHIC SONNETS

Fuente de la calle de la Hoguera

Tras las sombras de Ricardo
y los heraldos de entonces: Miguel,
Pablo, Juan, Mario, Julio and Rafael.

No nombraré la fuente ni la hoguera,
el ansia de los días compartidos
y esas horas del sol, pasos perdidos
tras el rumor oblicuo de la espera.

No diré la palabra prisionera
de un tiempo ya lejano, los latidos
mil veces refrenados, hoy heridos
irreparablemente. Mas quisiera

en el umbral del agua, en los jazmines
que columna custodian cual si fuera
ángel leve de besos y delfines,

detener el fulgor, decir cómo era
la soledad ayer, y los maitines.
Hay un misterio que callar debiera.

París, 21 de junio de 1983

Fountain in the Passage of the Bonfire

Under the shadows of Ricardo
and the heralds of that time: Miguel,
Pablo, Juan, Mario, Julio and Rafael.

I will not name the fountain nor the bonfire,
the longing for the shared days
and these sunny hours, footsteps lost
behind the oblique murmur of the wait.

I will not say the word prisoner
of a time already distant, the heartbeats
a thousand times restrained, hurt today
beyond repair. Yet I would love —

at the edge of water, in the jasmine
guarding the pillar as if it were
a light angel of kisses and dolphins —

to retain the splendor, to tell how yesterday's
solitude was, the matins.
There is a mystery I should keep secret.

Paris, 21 June 1983

También en soledad de amor herido

Al pintor Juan Alcalde

Juan de lumbre, de pan, de sol doliente.
Juan de miga y hogaza, Juan de luto.
Casi Juan panadero, Juan enjuto
como campo de trigo y de simiente.

Esplendor del sosiego, paz ardiente,
augurio indescifrable omen, signo y fruto,
homenaje a lo efímero y tributo
de polvo enamorado, encina o fuente.

Manantial es la vida o cautiverio
del hombre en soledad. Pensar, saberte
imagen del amor o cruel misterio.

Imagen del amor también la muerte
nos emplaza entre juncos. Baptisterio.
Gárgola esplendorosa o sueño inerte.

In Solitude Hurt by Love

To the painter Juan Alcalde

John of fire, of bread, of grieving sun.
John of crumb and large loaf, John of mourning.
John almost baker, John lean
like a wheat and seed field.

Quiet splendor, burning peace,
indecipherable omen, sign and fruit,
tribute to the ephemeral and sacrifice
enamored with ashes, oak or fountain.

Wellspring is life or captivity
for the man in solitude. To think, to know
yourself an image of love or cruel mystery.

Image of love too, death
finds us among reeds. Baptistry.
Splendid gargoyle or lifeless dream.

Entre las azucenas olvidado

Al pintor Miguel del Moral

Un cuchillo homicida de hoja larga
me busca el corazón arrebolado.
Buscadme el corazón, lo tengo a un lado
boca o herida audaz, sedienta, amarga.

Buscadme el corazón con una adarga
y lo hallaréis abierto, en flor granado
para el dolor crecido y madurado
como una fruta agraz de suave carga.

Tiene la espera olor de patio moro
y guitarras la noche y se despierta
mi corazón herido como un toro.

Herido como un toro en la reyerta
mi corazón astral, silbo sonoro
abre al amor de par en par la puerta.

Forgotten Amidst White Lilies

To the painter Miguel del Moral

A murderous long bladed saber
searches for my flushed heart.
Search for my heart, I have it on one side
like a bold mouth or wound, thirsty, bitter.

Search for my heart with a shield
and find it in bloom, fully opened
for sorrow grown and ripened
like a bitter fruit of mild weight.

The wait smells of Moorish courtyard
and the night of guitars and my heart
wakes like a wounded bull.

Wounded like a bull in battle
my astral heart, resounding whistle
opens the door wide to love.

Al pintor Pedro Bueno en Villa del Río

Arde el río, arde el mar,
humea el mundo.

— Luis de Góngora

Se elevarán las llamas hasta el cielo
incendiando la luz con su plegaria
y será su fulgor y luminaria
como un presagio oculto de tu vuelo.

Serafines y tronos en desvelo,
diamantes esculpidos, milenaria
concavidad del sol, incendiaria
teluridad opaca, ígneo hielo.

Has llevado el rigor hasta misterios
insondables de un arte sin ribera
abriendo al color blanco los cauterios

que nunca soñaría la Chimera.
Silente luz, arábigos sahumerios,
en tus manos pincel, pasión señera.

To the Painter Pedro Bueno in Villa del Río

Ablaze the rivers, ablaze the sea,
the world in smoke.

— Luis de Góngora

Flames ascend the sky,
prayers set fire to light,
their glow and illuminations
secretly announce your flight.

Seraphs and thrones in vigil,
sculpted diamonds, millennial
hollowness of the sun, incendiary
telluric opacity, igneous ice.

You pushed the rigor of a limitless art
to unfathomable mysteries
opening to the color white the singing

the Chimera never dreamt.
Occult light, impenetrable aromatic smoke,
in your paintbrush hands, solitary passion.

Elegía habitada

In memoriam Luis Cernuda

¿Quien, si gritara yo, me oiría
entre las legiones angélicas?

— Rainer Maria Rilke

A Pablo García Baena,
con quien tanto he querido

Te recuerdo por las calles de Viena.
En los amaneceres
tu recuerdo me viene a la memoria.
Cierro los párpados y me trasciende
el soplo de tu aliento, profecía
que en Delfos entendí, sobreviviendo
a una espera infinita.

Por las calles de Viena, tras el alba
de alhelíes en flor, tras los almendros
inalcanzables,
tras el fulgor alado de tus versos,
cierro los ojos y los abro
una y mil veces, para una y mil veces
recordar, para una y mil veces
despertar,
para una y mil veces hallar alivio,
abandonarme a tu custodia angélica,
cansado de llorar
por los que en tierra yacen.

Patria
tenemos en común y es el misterio.

Estaba escrito
sin que ni tú ni yo lo supieramos.

Inhabited Elegy

In memoriam Luis Cernuda

Who, if I cried out, would hear me
among the angelic legions?
— Rainer Maria Rilke

To Pablo García Baena,
with whom I shared so much

I remember you through the streets of Vienna.
In the sunrises
your memory comes back to me.
I close my eyes and the whiff
of your breath reaches me, prophecy
I grasped in Delphi, surviving
an infinite wait.

Through the streets of Vienna, past a dawn
of Erysimum in bloom, past unattainable
almond trees,
past the winged splendor of your verses,
I close my eyes and open them
a thousand and one times, to remember
a thousand and one times, to awake
a thousand and one times,
to find relief a thousand and one times,
to abandon myself to your angelic care,
weary of crying
for those who lie in the ground.

Homeland
we share and it is the mystery.

It was written
without you or I knowing it.

Tampoco fue el oráculo:
el índice de fuego que el destino
impone a veces en la frente
juvenil de los que ama,
un dios despiadado puso.

Caminante, a hombros llevas
esa alforja liviana, huella al fin
de ruiseñor ajeno al sacrificio.

Las sombras como bosques a tu conjuro
de árboles se pueblan y aparecen
los rostros habitados
de Hölderlin y Heráclito y la rosa
del epitafio aquel que desde Duino
sellaría en su tumba para siempre
el paso del poeta por la Tierra.

Oh luz incandescente
impenetrable luz embrigadora
en la noche perpetua que me habita
sin murmullos extraños ni tañidos
de campanas golosas.

Conmigo vas por las calles de Viena,
mi corazón habitas, el prodigio anuncias,
la majestad emplazas,
el aire hiendes que el amor respira
y te apartas de todo, invicto,
cubierto de saetas, trascendido,
ruiseñor inmolado
donde habita el olvido.

It wasn't the oracle either:
the forefinger of fire — that destiny
thrusts at times on the youthful
faces of those it loves —
a merciless god gave.

Traveler, you carry on your shoulders
this light knapsack, trace
at last of a nightingale alien to sacrifice.

The shadows like woods under your spell
fill with trees and the inhabited
faces of Hölderin and Heraclitus
appear and the rose
of that epitaph which since Duino
forever seals the grave
of the poet passing on Earth.

Oh incandescent light,
impenetrable intoxicating light
in the everlasting night that inhabits me
without strange whispers or the ringing
of greedy bells.

You go with me through the streets of Vienna,
you inhabit my heart, you announce the prodigy,
you summon majesty,
you cleave the air that love breathes
and you part from all, unconquered,
covered in sacred songs, illustrious,
nightingale immolated
where oblivion dwells.

Ruiseñor de la luz, prodigio alado,
déjame la canción que te llevaste
como un relevo olímpico. (Los bárbaros
arriaron sus enseñas y engendrando
están entre los muladares
como la lepra engendra. Miserere.)

La amapola risueña en tierra yerma
temblorosa lloró.
¿Quién dirá la desdicha,
quién puede recordar el alba incierta,
quién no se arrancará los ojos por no ver
tanta miseria atroz?

Las hoces, las guadañas, hasta los ríos
segaron. Alejémonos
sin volver la mirada. Ya no hay trigos
y solo camposantos, ni canciones
de gestas o de amor.
Llévame de la mano, peregrino,
oh penitente, y deja o abandona
tu mano como guante que resbale
entre mis manos y déjame
sentir cómo germina la semilla.

Florecerá el granado
donde dejes las huellas de tus pies.
Un fuego de alboradas
estallará en el cielo, cubrirá
la bóveda celeste.
Este cielo de Viena en noche clara
de plenilunio es ya el alba
del alhelí. (En Knossos, los delfines
saben como salir del Laberinto
y Teseo platica con Edipo
a sabiendas que el mar, destino último,

Nightingale of light, winged prodigy,
leave me the song you carried
like an Olympic relay. (The Barbarians
lowered their ensigns and they're
breeding in the dunghills
the way leprosy breeds. Miserere.)

The bright poppy wept
grieving in wasteland.
Who will say the calamity,
who can remember the inconstant sunrise,
who will not pluck out their eyes
so as not to see such atrocious misery?

The sickles, the scythes reaped
even the rivers. Let's move away
without looking back. There are no longer
wheat fields or love songs or epic poems,
only cemeteries.
Take me by the hand, pilgrim,
oh penitent, and leave or abandon
your hand like a glove slipping
through my hands and let me
feel how the seed germinates.

The pomegranate tree will bloom
where you leave your footprints.
A fire of aubades
will shatter the sky, covering
the firmament.
This Vienna sky in a clear full
moon night is already the dawn
of the Erysimum. (In Knossos, dolphins
know how to exit the Labyrinth
and Theseus chats with Oedipus
in full knowledge that the sea, final destiny,

su mortaja será. Porque los dioses
aman a los mortales y nosotros
pugnamos por volver al Laberinto.)

Dime tú que conoces el secreto
indescifrable de los signos,
dime tú con el signo de los ciegos
que no existe el reposo.

En nuestro breve espacio de vivos,
en nuestra soledad, ya poco queda.
Mas seguiré tu senda angosta
con la ilusión tenaz de quien se sabe
tan verdadero cuanto
esas voces anónimas que amamos
las del actor no son y lo que hacen
es prestar su antifaz al gesto eterno
del héroe, y éste, solo,
asumirá el papel de su destino.

Viena, 28 de septiembre de 1993

will be his shroud. Because the gods
love the mortals and we struggle
to return to the Labyrinth.)

Tell me, you who know
the undecipherable secret of signs,
tell me, you with the sign of the blind,
that repose doesn't exist.

In our brief time alive,
in our solitude, little is still left.
Yet I will follow your narrow path
with the stubborn illusion of someone
who knows himself as truthful
as these anonymous voices we love —
of the actor they are not — and what they do
is lend their masks to the eternal face
of the hero, and he alone
will take over the role of his destiny.

Vienna, 28 September 1993

Acknowledgments

I am deeply thankful to Andrés Neuman, Marsha de la O, Blas Falconer, Dorianne Laux, Christopher Merrill, Willis Barnstone, Daniel Simon, Robert Con Davis-Undiano, Michelle Johnson, Terri Stubblefield, Pedro Serrano, Ana Franco, Phil Taggart, Justin Bigos, Erin Stalcup, Anna Leahy, Claudia Serea, Loren Kleinman, Robert Nazarene, Daniel Lawless, Marc Vincenz, and Cathy Strisik.

I am incredibly grateful to Felip Cirer Costa and José Manuel Piña at *Diario de Ibiza*, Xicu Lluy at *Temps Moderns*, and Julio Herranz at *Ultima Hora Ibiza*.

Gracious thanks to Jessie Lendennie and Siobhán Hutson at Salmon Poetry for delivering this book into the world. And my endless gratitude to my angel John FitzGerald for all the magic.

Many thanks to the following Journals & Anthologies where many of the poems first appeared:

World Literature Today: "Tom Smithson Dead in his Garret," ed. Daniel Simon
Waxwing Literary Journal: "Montrouge Cemetery" and "Ibiza," eds. Justin Bigos & Erin Stalcup
Periódico de Poesía: "El Embeleso," "Tom Smithson muerto en su buhardilla," eds. Pedro Serrano and Ana Franco
Askew Poetry Journal: "From the Euxine Sea," eds. Marsha de la O & Phil Taggart
Plume Poetry Journal: "Poem to Circe IV" and "Fountain in the Passage of the Bonfire," ed. Daniel Lawless
National Translation Month: "Inhabited Elegy," "From the Euxine Sea," "Poem to Circe II," and "Poem to Circe XII," eds. Claudia Serea & Loren Kleinman
The London Magazine: "Poem to Circe XIX," ed. Steven O'Brien
The American Journal of Poetry: "Poem to Circe III," "Poem to Circe IX," "Poem to Circe XV," "Poem to Circe XVII," "Poem to Circe XVIII," and "To the Painter Pedro Bueno in Villa del Río," ed. Robert Nazarene
TAB: The Journal of Poetry & Poetics: "The Spell," ed. Anna Leahy
Taos Journal of International Poetry & Art: "Forgotten Amidst White Lilies," "The Man and the Stone" and "Poem to Circe XX," eds. Cathy Strisik & Veronica Golos
The Plume Anthology of Poetry 3: "Ode to a Young Mariner," ed. Daniel Lawless
The Plume Anthology of Poetry 5: "In Solitude Hurt by Love," ed. Daniel Lawless
The Plume Anthology of Poetry 6: "Poem to Circe XII," ed. Daniel Lawless

JOSÉ MANUEL CARDONA is a poet, writer and translator from Ibiza, Spain. He is the author of *El Vendimiador* (Atzavara, 1953), *Poemas a Circe* (Adonais, 1959), and *El Bosque de Birnam: Antología poética* (Consell Insular d'Eivissa, 2007), published as a tribute by the government of Ibiza.

He co-founded and co-edited several literary journals, among them *Luna Negra*, with José María Rodriguez Méndez, and *Atzavara*, with Francisco Galí, and wrote for many publications (*Cántico, Ibiza, Isla, Eivissa, Caracola, Arkángel, Alcaraván, Poesía Española, Azemar, Alfoz, Trilce, La Calandria, Aljaba, Mensaje*, among others). He participated in the II Congreso de Poesía in Salamanca and belonged to the Cántico group.

The Franco regime forced him into exile in France. Years later, when the socialists came to power in Spain, he was offered a ministry position, which was ultimately denied him by the still heavily embedded Franquist administration. (He remained blacklisted for several years).

He holds PhDs in literature and humanities (University of Nancy), and political sciences (Graduate Institute of International and Development Studies, Geneva). He wrote his thesis on the Mexican revolution at the Instituto de Cultura Hispánica de Madrid and is an attorney (University of Barcelona).

He worked for the United Nations most of his life, in Geneva, Paris, Rome, Vienna, Belgrade, Sofia, Kiev, Tbilisi, Moscow, St. Petersburg, and Panama, among many places.

HÉLÈNE CARDONA is the author of seven books, most recently *Life in Suspension, Dreaming My Animal Selves*, and the translations *Beyond Elsewhere* (Gabriel Arnou-Laujeac), winner of a Hemingway Grant, *Ce que nous portons* (Dorianne Laux); and *Whitman et La Guerre de Sécesssion*: Walt Whitman's *Civil War Writings* for WhitmanWeb.

She has translated Rimbaud, Baudelaire, René Depestre, Ernest Pépin, Aloysius Bertrand, Maram Al-Masri, Eric Sarner, Jean-Claude Renard, Nicolas Grenier, Christiane Singer, and John Ashbery. Publications include *Washington Square Review, World Literature Today, Poetry International, The London Magazine, The Brooklyn Rail, Hayden's Ferry Review, Drunken Boat, Anomaly, Asymptote*, and *The Warwick Review*.

She worked as a translator/interpreter for the Canadian Embassy in Paris, received fellowships from the Goethe-Institut and the Universidad Internacional de Andalucía, the 2017 International Book Award in Poetry, the 2017 Best Book Award in Poetry, the 2015 USA Best Book Award in Poetry, 2 Pinnacle Book Awards for the Best Bilingual Poetry Book, and 2 Readers' Favorite Book Awards in Poetry.

Hélène has served as a judge for the 2017 Jacar Press Full Length Competition, the 2016 PEN Center USA Translation Award, the 2015 Writer's Digest Challenge, and the 2014 Rabindranath Tagore Award. She co-edits *Plume, Fulcrum*, and *Levure Littéraire*.

Acting credits include *Chocolat, Jurassic World, Dawn of the Planet of the Apes, The Hundred-Foot Journey, Serendipity, Mumford* & more.

www.salmonpoetry.com

Like the sea-run Steelhead salmon that thrashes upstream to its spawning ground, then instead of dying, returns to the sea — Salmon Poetry Press brings precious cargo to both Ireland and America in the poetry it publishes, then carries that select work to its readership against incalculable odds.

TESS GALLAGHER